T0149377

On The Healing Road
Through The Eyes
Of An Adoptee

Poems Of Inspiration And Hope

The Poet Dena

authorHOUSE®

AuthorHouse™
1663 Liberty Drive
Bloomington, IN 47403
www.authorhouse.com
Phone: 1 (800) 839-8640

Published by AuthorHouse 11/30/2018

ISBN: 978-1-5462-6875-8 (sc)
ISBN: 978-1-5462-6874-1 (e)

Print information available on the last page.

Any people depicted in stock imagery provided by Getty Images are models, and such images are being used for illustrative purposes only. Certain stock imagery © Getty Images.

This book is printed on acid-free paper.

Contents

Assorted Poetry

Adoption

Issues

Being An Adult Child

I often appear so immature
I act in childish ways
For even though my body aged
My mind stuck in younger days

When I was just a little girl
About the age of eight
I felt I had to be mature
My childhood had to wait

So much responsibility
So strong I had to be
No opportunity was there
To be playful or carefree

The years passed by eventually
I did what was required
And then one day I realized
That all I felt was very tired

I look like I'm an Adult
Who has managed to survive
But inside I'm just a child
Who needs to feel alive

So many things left unresolved
The questions and the fears,
The hidden feelings that I dread
Even after 50 years

The world I knew has ended
A new mission's drawing near
If I can heal the little "Me"
Sounds of happiness I will hear

Though no one really understands
"You've got it made," they say
"To pick and choose what ever you want.
You can have it your own way!"

How I wish it were so easy
I'm not used to being Boss!
I need to have a purpose
Without guidance I am lost

For the first time someone's asked
"What do you want to do?"
I answer, "How should I know?
For me this is so new!"

You must investigate your passions
Allow all past hurts to heal
Create a bond with Spirit
It's time that you felt real

Just focus on your feelings
Let experience help you grow
With lots of love and patience
Soon your true path you will know

It's not like in the movies
Blink your eyes and you are whole
It's a long and tedious journey
Repairing the injuries to my soul

Deep In Our Hearts

What does the word Adoption mean?
Depends on your point of view
To some, the parting of two hearts
But the joining of two hearts too

It starts off with a trauma
A young girl left confused
A new life in the balance
Two different paths to choose

"If I were to keep the baby
Only HIS (father's) face I would see
'Tis better for all concerned
With a new family he/she should be"

Some birth family is supportive
"It's only a baby, nothing more"
But others try to convince her
Raising a child's a very big chore

Decision time is now at hand
The choice is hers to make
Not used to thinking of herself
Only one road she can take

Both mom and child are told to
Forget about what's occurred
Just pretend it never happened
Bury deep the grief procured

Immersed in either joy or pain
Life simply carries on
Two souls with missing pieces
Often cry from dusk till dawn

Down deep within the silence
Where no one else can see
Hide dreams and hopes and nightmares
One day together they will be

They both fear that hate and anger
Will colour what they'd say
They pray that joy and understanding
Be the one's to rule the day

That young girl's now a woman
With more children, most likely not
Even with each passing decade
Her firstborn she's not forgot

The child has built a new world
Doting parents who are the best
Though her roots remain a mystery
Surviving rejection's the real test

Both mom and child have "adopted"
Society's biased point of view,
"Be grateful for what transpired
'Twas a blessing that happened to you!"

They both play at being happy
It's but a mask they hide behind
But the secret grief and longing
Allude to answers they must find

And on their arduous journey
Daring to dream and pray
Of their two hearts reunited
And healed that miraculous day

For Their Love

"Now you be a "good girl"
I've heard this all my life
Whether I be their daughter,
Her mother, his wife.

I believed I had to please them
My responsibility, my duty, my role
But to my surprise, between them,
'Twas my free will that they stole

And then one day when I awoke
I found to my dismay
They all no longer needed me
They all had gone away

My parents had got sick and died
My daughter, she was grown
My husband seemed a stranger to me
Help! I cannot function on my own!

I have no reason to get up
There's no one left to serve
I have no purpose for my life
Where's the reverence I deserve?

The myth that I grew up with
"If you give you shall receive"
But I've given till I am empty
When will They give love to Me?

Without them I am nothing
I don't think that I exist
Only their love gave me substance
It vanished with their last kiss

But my life is hardly over
I'm only "middle age"
Although I sacrificed my soul
It's time to turn the page

For all the tears and all the pain
A new life I must try
'Cause instead of "being chosen"
Only I now choose! That's why!

Given Away

"You're going to a new home
You're going there today
They're going to love you so much."
That's what I heard her say.

She sounded oh so cheerful
Like this is something good
It seems I should be happy
I think you thought I would.

I'm going to live with strangers
And they live far away!
You say that they'll be nice to me
But I just want to stay!

You used to say you loved me
But now I'm filled with fear
Did I do something wrong
That you don't want me here?

I thought we'd be together
Forever and always
Explain to me the reason
We must be parting ways.

I thought that we belonged
Together all our days!
But then you said to go with them
You so easily gave me away!

Oh, how my heart is breaking
I'm puzzled and confused
If you can do this thing to me
Can not they do it too?

Goodbye to all that I hold dear!
My tears are coming fast!
I think that I might actually die!
Will this feeling ever pass?

How can I ever trust again?
Why must this torture be?
Can I believe the words I'm told
When THEY say they love me?

I feel like a possession
Just passed from hand to hand
But I'm a living, feeling being
I just can't understand

That I could just be given away
Abandoned and rejected
Like some old piece of furniture
You hardly seemed affected

You were not worthy of my love!
I tell myself, once more!
To have given it away so easily
Is that all it's good for?!

So very many years have passed
And still I sit and wonder
My curious Inner Child just asked
Is giving (being given) really better?

God's Little Angel

Where did I come from?
How did I come to be?
Who were my parents?
Why won't you please tell me?

How was I growing up?
Was I fast or was I slow?
When did I start to walk and talk?
Why is it I don't know?

What were my first words?
Did I laugh or did I cry?
I have so many questions
And no one to answer me – WHY?

Why is my past a secret?
Is it something really bad?
I've grown up without knowing
And it makes me very sad!

I'm just a child who wants the truth,
How horrible could it be?
Why must you be mysterious?
This says so much to me!

I have no sense of who I am,
Of being born or wanted.
Why am I not to know the facts?
Must my infancy remain haunted?

I'm told all children come from God,
His Angels made from love.
If that's the case, then answer me,
So my birth self I can love.

Not Mine

Even after all these years
You still can break my heart
It only takes four little words
To tear my world apart

I thought, at last, I knew the truth
All secrets were revealed
I'd put the past behind me
Most of its pain was healed

And then you said those awful words
They cut me to the bone
For once again I'm being denied
Feeling abandoned and alone

How could you be so cruel to me?
My dreams had turned out fine
I was so happy and content
'Till you claimed "YOU ARE NOT MINE!"

One Precious Moment

"Would you do it all again?"
Is a question I am asked
"Was it worth all of the pain?"
The price of digging up the past

"Oh God! Yes!" was my reply
Without thought or hesitation
Though the work itself was hard
It was the source of my salvation

The journey started long ago
And plagued me all my life
I feared there were no answers
That only death would end my strife

The warnings came from all around
"Your dreams will not come true!"
Maybe only nightmares I will find
But I must do what I must do

Please understand it is my right
My God has told me so
To comprehend where I come from
I will not stop until I know

My journey lasted 50 years
With so many stops and starts
But in the end, a precious gift
It was the healing of our hearts

That fateful day was surely blessed
Full of wonders for Mom and Me
To see each other face to face
Was believed impossible to be

She never even saw it coming
She didn't even have a clue
Then I said, "I am your first-born
I want to say that I LOVE YOU!"

She looked at me in disbelief
For this came out of the blue
Then tenderly she hugged me
And said, "I LOVE YOU TOO!"

We sat together, side by side
One precious moment stuck in time
As I lovingly gazed into her eyes
And she lovingly gazed into mine

The unconditional love I felt
Spirit answering both our prayers
I felt a lifetime of sorrow and pain
Evaporate and release me, then and there

Reunion

I got that wondrous phone call
The one I dreamt about for years
The precious child I gave away
Is reaching out, in spite of fear

Of once again being rejected
Dreading what I'll say or do
I really want her to understand
I am having these fears too!

My heart's pounding in my chest
My stomach's tied in a knot
What will she think when she sees me?
Will she be angry, pleased, or not?

I want so much to meet her
Look into her dazzling eyes
To feel her arms embrace me
Separate truth from all the lies

That I've been forced to believe
Permitting me to carry on
Can I overcome the mental terror
And claim the prize I've won?

For the birth mom, prayers answered
A voice out of the past
A lost child, gone but not forgot
Part of her soul restored at last

An end to all the wondering
Unanswered questions, guilt and shame
Those Heavenly words, "I LOVE YOU, MOM!
AND HOPE YOU FEEL THE SAME!"

For the adopted child, journey's end
A family history now complete
Exchanging fantasy for truth
A mirror image – oh, so sweet!

All the knowledge she has sought
From the time she ascertained
That to others she was connected
An improved self-image has been gained

The missing pieces they both sought
That empty hole in both their hearts
The anguish of a lifetime
Now fades as the healing starts

I know that whatever the outcome
They'll both remember this special day
The moment they first saw each other
Just proves "where there's a will there IS a way!"

To Know The Truth

Oh! How important 'twas to know
My mothers story, good and bad
All those many years ago
Then I wouldn't have been so sad

If only I had had some proof
Some object of hers, some possession
Then maybe I'd have been content
Instead of living with an obsession

I wish everyone would understand
This need is quite instinctive
For you to share information would be
The best treasure you could give

Instead of living with the fantasies
Both nightmarish and sublime
To know the truth would have allowed
For a healthier way to bide my time

How wonderful it would have been
To have made that spiritual connection
My soul then would have been at peace
And my heart able to receive affection

It always hurt me, oh so much
Your secrets and your lies
For if you could not accept her
Part of me, too, you must despise

I need for you to realize
That if you truly do love me
This saying really does ring true
THE TRUTH SHALL SET YOU (Me) FREE!

Who's My Mom

"She is not your REAL mom
She just gave birth to you
'Twas I that spent all night and day
Through measles, cold, and flu"

At first this seemed to satisfy
The curious little child
But in later years this quandary
Would almost drive me wild

Soon she was old enough to ask
"How did I come to be?
Did I grow inside your tummy?
How was it you picked me?"

"Alas, I was unable
To have kids of my own
So I signed up with the agency
And then sat by the phone

One day there came that special call
We've a perfect child for you
She's oh so cute and full of life
And she's only turning two!"

Whose tummy did I come out of?
Was it from my foster mom?
Was it from her body I was born?
NO! You mean I have a THIRD mom!!

"But I'm the only one who counts
For I've been here all along
The others now must take their place
In the past where they belong"

What do I think about them?
What is it that I feel?
They who went out of my life
Why imply that they're unreal?

This is my understanding
Of what I knew to be true
We got you from your Foster mom
But you had a Birth mom too

Both of them did love me?
But both gave me away!
Maybe the problem lies with me
That they did not want me to stay?

If they were not my REAL moms
Is not part of me unreal?
Do you have ANY idea
How confused this makes me feel?

How can it be, are opposites both true?
Did I ever grieve those that I lost?
Did I not exist before the age of two?
Secrets kept, no matter what the cost?

How could you really expect me
To believe the accounts you told
They were nothing more than fairy tales
All my fears were put on hold

A child can't deal with endless worry
Scary thoughts, feelings suppressed
"When I become a mature adult
The answers will not be repressed!"

If only I could have known
Then what I know today
My confidence and sense of worth
Would not have been thrown away

I want you all to understand
Those words cut like a knife
ALL of these mothers are genuine
ALL had a role in my life

They ALL make up a part of me
Of the person I've become
Let me cherish each relationship
For I love them, EVERY ONE!

Emotional
Issues

Buried Feelings

I went looking for my feelings
But they were nowhere to be found
I forgot where I had buried them
So deeply hidden, far underground.

I took a guess and started digging
But much to my dismay
I came upon a mighty vault
The sign said: STOP – GO AWAY

"Advance at your own peril,"
Someone inside me said.
"Beyond here hides a mined maze.
WATCH OUT – OR YOU'LL BE DEAD"

"But I FEEL that way already,"
Was my answer to the voice.
"And if I am to feel alive,
I really have no choice."

That's when I heard the warning growls
They froze me in my tracks.
Glaring eyes inside dark shadows.
"DANGER AHEAD – BETTER TURN BACK"

"We're powerful and angry beasts.
Too long we've been restrained.
Release us out into the light.
Never again will we be chained"

"I am not your enemy,
Someone that you must fear"
"You're the one that locked us up,
The one who put us here"

"There was no choice," was my reply,
"For I was but a child.
Filled with doubt and scared to death
No way could you run wild"

"So you think now that time has passed
You have the right to pry
Into our safe, protected world
All we can ask is WHY?"

"I know that I have hurt you
And your anger is justified
But I have also paid a price
We must both put the past aside."

"Why is it we should trust you?
What do we have to gain?"
"The answer's very simple, you see
ONLY I CAN STOP THE PAIN"

"The offer's very tempting and yet
We want to run and hide."
"Please, just give me one more chance!"
"Well, okay, proceed inside"

The vault door sprang wide open
My heart began to pound
The moment of truth had just arrived
And this is what I found

A multitude of padlocked doors
Of various strengths and sizes
Maybe I should pick a small one
That would seem to be the wisest

The first beasts, they were easy
So much anger, so much pain
Though 'twas scary to confront them
So afraid I'd go insane

"Take baby steps, that's how to start
A little bit at a time.
Their power's not so strong that way
Let's proceed, you're doing fine"

"Invite the feelings to come out,"
The voice inside me said.
But they were now the stronger ones
I met their rage with dread.

Their power and strength surprised me
At times I'd want to flee.
But soon I came to realize
A wonderful calmness grew in me.

It's taken 4 years, I've worked real hard
To tame the beasts inside
So many now have been released
And I know where the others hide

Casualty of War

The war, it was now over
And the dreams were all dead
My victory felt hollow
All the wounds were in my head

No longer need I answer
To all of their demands
Through strength of will and anger
My life's back in my own hands

The battle scars are many
My soul has paid the price
For every loss and win
Hope vanquished not once but twice

Outwardly I'm a trooper
Who's so competent and wise
But hiding on the inside is
Another "me" wearing a disguise

She's oh so lost and weary
Struggle started long ago
How to now begin a new life
When sacrifice is all I know?

To others I look normal
They do not see my pain
Puzzled by my reactions
"You have no cause to complain!"

That's why I envy veterans
With physical injuries
They have no need to justify
Coping with emotional disease

Recovery time is expected
There's help at every turn
Unlike the unsung hero
Who's just left to crash and burn

No parades or ribbons exist
To honor what I've endured
The false "me" everyone saw
Has been killed instead of cured

Now all that is remaining
Is the little Me that's hid
She must pick up the pieces
Though "middle aged" she feels a kid

Again she faces danger
And dread at every turn
These fiends are quite personal
As she is quick to learn

Now a new war's before me
Make these demons disappear
When at last I'm triumphant
No more struggle, no more fear

Give Up Your Dreams And Die

I remember the moment well
The night I emotionally died
I put my dreams on hold
And everyday since I've cried

I played the game for 30 years
I dutifully carried on
Ignorant of the consequences
My soul felt preyed upon

A lonely little girl
Just wanting to belong
Becomes a haunted woman
Feeling weak instead of strong

She's been on auto-pilot
Lost and numb on the inside
Wondering where the joy went
Swept away by the tearful tide

Then one day all the illusions
And world come crashing down
The reasons I died no longer exist
But now my dreams cannot be found

How to bring them back to life
Now that I'm middle aged?
Is it even possible to revive
What has been disengaged?

I don't truly remember how
It feels to fantasize
I dwelt so long in darkness
The sunlight's painful to my eyes

I struggle to reconnect to
What was buried so long ago
Back to my child-like heart and soul
To the sense of hope I used to know

Glorious Release

What is this feeling concealed inside
All pent up and confined?
Emotions and notions secluded
They've been long ago left behind

The pressure mounts as time goes by
I think I'm going to burst
From the anguish and the woe
It's peace for which I thirst

Who can I confess to when
There's no one I can trust?
A need to bare my very soul
Buried under layers of dust

How to withstand the onslaught
Erupting now from within
A volcano ready to explode
I'm overcome by the din

The silent screams, the hopeless grief,
The never-ending tears
Threatening to blow up the dam
And expose all of my fears

I'm choked up and exhausted
And drowning in the surge
My heart and mind are pounding
Past ghosts yearning to emerge

An avalanche of feelings
Comes bursting through the door
As waves of suffering and sorrow
Like a lion, start to roar

From deep down in the darkness
My spirit's long-held pain
A multitude of wordless thoughts
Take up a new refrain

At last the healing has begun
Though the process takes its toll
My inner resolve is crumbling
Finding closure is my goal

I'm light-headed from my happiness
And the shock of new-found bliss
With a voice no longer silent
I'm so amazed I survived this

I Am Afraid

The little child inside of me
Is cowering and afraid
She cannot find the courage to break
The secret pact she made.

"I promised I would not reveal
Those wicked things I think
To do so would be deadly
Though at times I'm on the brink."

"Oh! Little one, do not despair
Your thoughts are not so bad
There's no one left you need to fear
Tell me why you're so sad."

"There's no one to protect me
From the monsters that I fear
No matter how I try to hide
What if they find me here?

Perhaps they're going to kill me!
Or worse, claim that I'm theirs!
Oh! Lord, please tell me what to do
And please stop my nightmares!

I'm timid, shy, and oh so scared
And yet I long to tell
The secrets that I've locked inside
And break their evil spell"

"Just realize you're safe right now
Here in this "special" place
Stay in this moment and you'll find
They're not so hard to face"

"Oh! No!" I cried, "I'm petrified
I cannot face their wrath!
I fear they will devour me
If I dare to cross their path

I've dreaded them for far too long
I yielded to their demands"
"But that was when you were so small
Now, I can help you take a stand

Your feelings are neither right nor wrong
They want only to be expressed.
Together we can tame the beasts
All you need do is try your best"

"Oh! How I pray that you are right
That your promises do come true
What I wouldn't give to be free of fear
And my world to be anything but blue"

I Am Angry

So many hidden emotions
Buried deep within the past
I found a gentle guide
To help uncover them, at last

Focus on the strongest one
The easiest to attain
Think about that little girl
And tap into her pain

She asks "What do you feel?"
And the answer's right there
I scream "I AM ANGRY!"
The shout makes her stare.

Then she asks "What about?"
And again it's so clear
"ABOUT SO MANY THINGS"
I yell in her ear!

"Oh how am I angry
Let me count the ways
The list is quite long
I could go on and on for days

Let's start with the Lord
For He is the first
I feel He's abandoned me
What else could be worse?

Next come my parents
I'm on my third set
They love then reject me
Not much more than a pet

They say tell the truth
Then they tell me a lie
They say, "Don't ask questions!"
But each time I ask WHY?

My peers all rebuff me
They just call me names
You're so crazy and weird
Were some of their claims

The world makes me angry
So hostile, so cold
It's a very scary place
When you're not very old

My past is a secret
I've no right to know
"Just trust what we tell you."
To that I say NO!

How blind can you be
To the pain I am in?
And why do I pay
For someone else's sin?

The fault was not mine!
I cry in the night
Why isn't life fair?
Please make it all right!

My dreams are so many
My needs are so few
But I feel I have no one
That I can tell them to

There's no one to listen
There's no one I trust
But I want to express them
I know that I must

Why do they reject me?
Why don't I belong?
Have I really been cursed?
How could they be wrong?

How will I survive?
Why does life go on?
If I last long enough
Will this anger be gone?

The tears fall like raindrops
Tell me what can I do?"
"My dear! I'm so sorry!
Now I'm angry too!"

Loneliness

Tell me the meaning, you ask
But how can you comprehend
What it's like to feel
Solitude without an end?

For me the answer's easy
It's the story of my life
Though outwardly I wear a smile
I've endured a lot of strife

For me it started early
When I was just a child
The sadness and the pain
They nearly drove me wild

There were secrets to be kept
Feelings and thoughts unexpressed
It made me seem an alien
All my life I've been depressed

I believed that God had cursed me
Though why I did not know
Alone in a hostile world
My broken heart could not show

Many a night my tears fell
As silently I cried
When despair would overcome me
Till I wished that I had died

There were times I hid in numbness
Some peace I hoped to find
Though my victory was hollow
To all around me I was blind

I shut down so completely
As the years did pass me by
I resigned to just endure
Though I never stopped asking Why?

Are there no other creatures
Who are the same as me?
If all beings are created
Then how did I come to be?

By all logic there must be
Some others of my own kind
But no matter how hard I look
Not a single one can I find

No acceptance, never feeling safe
In this universe I did dwell
In order to know true loneliness
You must first spend time in Hell!

My Inner Children

The answer to the problem
Was a little hard to see
But one day I became aware
Of many children within me

They were all of different ages
And each had their own name
The issues and concerns they had
Revolved around fear and shame

The question then arises
How did they come to be?
I guess it's 'cause I've always felt
Emotionally abused, you see.

My job was now to make contact
With each and every one
And lead them from the darkness
And help them find the sun

Dina is the baby
Her age from birth to two
She's very scared and insecure
And starved for attention too

She's taken to a new home
And given a new name
She cannot speak, she can't explain
"I'm alarmed by so much change!"

Pammy is the toddler
Her age is two to five
She's the one with all the hope
And glad to be alive

She's getting all the things she wants
Attention, toys, and clothes
But there is something missing
Yet her pain, it never shows

My childhood name is Pamela
It covers six to thirteen
Now's when the trauma truly starts
The worst it's ever been

All her questions go unanswered
Her peers just call her names
Her anger and pain grow day by day
Why does she always get the blame?

She can no longer tolerate
The silence and the fears
She buries them inside herself
Where they'll hide for many years

I changed my name to Pam
When fourteen I did turn
Feeling sinful, weird, and rejected
These were her main concerns

The years have passed at last
And physically they have grown
But each child still is frozen
Each needs attention all her own

I start at the beginning
With Dina first I walk
She communicates with gestures
It's hard for her to talk

I tell her that I love her
I can feel her in my heart
I know her thoughts, I know her fears
Never again will we be apart

As I take her in my arms
The world around us blurs
And as I kiss and dry her tears
A miracle occurs

There's a sudden understanding
No longer are we blue
I swear it happened just that fast
Then we were one instead of two!

Inspired, I turned to Pammy
"Join us," was my request.
For if we can work together
The outcome will be best

'Cause Pammy had the verbal skills
For Dina she could speak
It was easy now to understand
Why both of them felt weak

It took us some time
But with patience and love
We found our spiritual guidance,
Guardian Angels sent from above

Pamela has been watching us
But it's hard for her to trust
So many times she's felt betrayed
"But I'll join you if I must."

"Please take your time," we say to her
"Just do the best you can.
Try little steps until you learn
To be your greatest fan"

This process takes a long time
With hard work you'll discover
All those terrifying secrets
You can finally uncover.

Last but not least there is Pam
Who feels that she's not real
Merely an outward manifestation,
An android unable to feel

To her I must give my compassion
"Without you I would not have survived
And though your life was full of strife
I am grateful to still be alive."

I gather up my children
"I'm so proud of you all!
You've been so brave and patient
You've knocked down all the walls!"

So, now we have each other
To comfort and help grow
And each day we are learning
How to share all that we know

Pain-filled Connections

Where does all the pain go
That hides quietly away?
Waiting oh so patiently
To be released one day

A jumble of mixed feelings
Needing to be revealed
But there's no one to listen
And so our fate is sealed

It resides in the muscles
Often giving rise to cramps
In headaches and in nightmares
Pillows tear-filled and damp

The scared little girl
Sure they won't understand
Finds relief in the numbness
Too timid to take a stand

And as the years pass
Unmourned grief turns to rage
As more and more hurts
Are compounded with age

She's now an adult
But her problem's the same
Out of touch with her body
Repressed feeling mixed with shame

I think part of the problem is
She can't let go the past
The pain keeps her connected
Afraid the memories won't last

That without all the sorrow
She'd have severed the link
To issues and events and
Those lost in a blink

"Cause she'd made sacrifices
Putting her life on hold
Believing that in the future
All the answers would unfold

The reasons for endless suffering
The brutal heartache she'd endured
When daily putdowns became routine
Would her wounded soul ever be cured?

A recent loss triggers an onslaught
Of anger, betrayal, and guilt
A vital piece of her is missing
Her "punish-meter" goes to "TILT"

As the ghosts line up in front of her
She's resistant to saying "good-bye"
She feels somehow she failed them
In anguish she asks God "Why?"

Spirit answered her so tenderly
'Twas simply just their time
Instead of dwelling on their passing
Focus on them in their prime

The love you had, it lives on still
Each time you call their name
Bonds once forged cannot be broke
Part of an eternal flame

Know that you made a difference
As you received so did you give
It's only by honouring your losses
That you can show you've even lived

Secrets

Hush now, Baby! Don't say a word!
You must keep inside
The questions and the feelings
That forever you must hide

Expected to always play the game
In silence and loyalty
Warned of grievous consequence
If somebody should see

The turmoil and the anguish
Concealed behind thick walls
Must not look them in the eye
Lest even one wall falls

Confused and so determined
Never ever to betray
I promise to keep the secrets
Until my dying day!

How to keep on functioning?
To do the daily tasks
I construct an inner dungeon
And hide behind many masks

Outwardly I stay the same
So no one else will guess
The sadness hidden deep within
And the depth of my loneliness

As months turn into years
My desperation grows
My little child can't tolerate
The fear that overflows

Promises of dire punishments
Unspoken yet understood
Overcome by fantasies
I solemnly promise to be "good"

Self-image lies in shatters
I cry most every night
Through nightmares never ending
All alone with my plight

I'm used to keeping to myself
My spirit's paid the price
Of secrets kept for 50 years
Relief would sure be nice

No more mental torture, no chains
Weighted in the past
But even when it's offered
I can't believe it'll last

My 4 little inner-children
Each frozen in their youth
Cautiously at first reveal
Their versions of the truth

At first, just a small grievance
They tremble as they wait
Imagining the very worst
What is to be their fate?

Will the world come to an end?
Will God now strike them dead?
The gracious silence engulfs them
Calming their fears and dread

The journey takes about 5 years
A scary roller coaster ride
To purge most of the secrets
And give my soul some pride

In my stamina and endurance
Through emotional distress
The heart-felt poems that I write
Secrets I can NOW express

Soul Pain

I speak about intense pain
That tears apart the soul
It crushes hope and faith
And obliterates the whole

Impossible to imagine
'Til you meet it face to face
But the moment leaves you numb
All feeling gone, without a trace

I endured this very plight
First when I was just a child
Then again when I was grown
Both times it drove me wild

I placed the blame on God
Was convinced that I was cursed
Wouldn't wish this on my enemy
Even if he was my worst

In solitude I suffered
The wounds were all inside
My nightmares went unnoticed
In fantasies I chose to hide

Lost and alone in your world
I had none of my own
Just overwhelming childhood fears
That chilled me to the bone

I found it hard to comprehend
I was not the only one
It hurts to picture others
To whom this too was done

If I could open up and share
The secrets I still keep
Perhaps I'd save our lost souls
For together we could weep

How do we find each other?
I'm praying for a clue
It will take all of my strength
To get this message out to you!

The Me You Don't See

I live in the darkness
I cry silent tears
I'm shouting out words
That nobody hears

There's a pain in my heart
That lies shattered in pieces
Although it's still beating
The suffering never ceases

There's a hole in my soul
No words can describe IT
The best I can conjure
Is a dark bottomless pit

I hide behind masks
So no one will see
The sadness and sorrow
That live within me

I'm outwardly cheerful
I play the game well
I must not give clues
That inside I'm in Hell

My world has just ended
It's been torn apart
They say "go on living"
But how do I start?

Not able to trust
My solitude's complete
The silence is deafening
I gracefully accept defeat

All those I have loved
Have died or moved on
I've no one to care for
Now that they're all gone

What purpose to life when
There's no one but me?
It's Your help I require
A new future to see

To live or to die!
That's the choice I must make
I'm praying for guidance
Which path do I take?

I will NOT go on
With this anguish and pain
It's Your strength that I need
To start over again

Once more I'm aware
Of His voice in my head
"There's no turning back
If you chose to be dead!

To you I have given
All you need in this life;
The strength to endure,
A strong will to survive."

Many times have I wondered,
"Are these things a curse?"
He answers; "Oh, No!!
Or life would be so much worse"

Unexpressed Grief

Where do these feelings come from?
Why do they trouble me?
What problems must I work on
In order to be free?

I've always felt so helpless
I've no say in my life
What I want doesn't matter
My world seems full of strife.

In silence do I battle
With questions left unanswered.
There's no one I can talk to
All avenues are hampered

I'm lethargic and exhausted
And worn out from the fight
All alone do I struggle
But still no end's in sight

My sadness overwhelms me
As does my guilt and shame
Did I sin when I was little?
Is that why I'm in pain?

I lost so much so early
My parents, history, and name
From others I am different
Even though I look the same

There's an emptiness inside of me
Nowhere do I belong
But I must keep on searching
It's hard to always be strong!

My sorrow grows throughout the years
Once just sad, I'm now depressed
I want to die, my woes to end
Perhaps then I can rest?

I'm so surprised to learn the truth
About what these feelings mean
They represent my inner torment
That for too long has been unseen.

This sadness needs to be expressed
And brought out into the light
For then the grief can start to heal
A healthier future's now in sight

HEALING
AND
HOPE

Acknowledgment

I had dwelt upon my anger
Why had they been so mean?
How could I ever tell them
How frightening they did seem?

I tried to find the right words
For feelings held inside
Some way to simply say
All that I'd had to hide

It was now time to express
The lessons I had learned
To show them the compassion
And forgiveness they had earned

I did this undertaking for
My parents and for me
So from a troubled past
I could finally be free

As I sat out in the sunshine
Calming nature all around
I wrote a letter to my folks
About the wisdom I had found

At first my little child cried out
She couldn't wait to vent
A lifetime of pain and loneliness
The heartache through which she'd went

But then the more adult me
Who had by now begun to heal
Stated her enlightened view
About a different way to feel

Regarding past behavior
A mature understanding
Of events from long ago
Now a tribute could I sing

One day many months later
I knew the moment was right
The time for closure had arrived
I never dreamt I'd feel so light

I laid my plan out carefully
Imagined all that I would do
Though the sky was dark and cloudy
To my needs I did stay true

At their graveside near the fence
With a balloon that held my note
I repeated each and every word
As skyward I watched it float

The final words I said out loud
'Twas a testament to my love
A prayer that they'd both found
Peace and happiness up above

After I was several blocks away
I decided to look back and
Much to my surprise I saw
That the sky was no longer black

Instead over the cemetery
Twice as wide as it should be
Was a hole among the clouds
A special message meant just for me.

Beams of light were shining down
As I was overcome by awe
They had received my message
It was their answer that I saw

They were telling me unmistakably
They were pleased with what I'd done
And even Spirit was overjoyed
That I had forgiven everyone

A Healing Retreat

One day we came together
Our secret lives to share
We were six different souls
With many woes to bare

Some of us have met before
Some of us are new
But there are similar feelings
That we have all been through

It takes us all some time
We know to start out slow
Building up our confidence
As the grueling hours go

One by one we opened up
Facing our fears and concerns
The others, identifying with our plight
Gave the support for which we yearn

Now we are no longer silent
Our voices we've discovered
With beating drums, an anger dance,
Hidden feelings are uncovered

By the end of the day
With new skills acquired
We all felt much stronger,
Peaceful, confident, and inspired

A Hospital of Love

What if there was such a place?
Safe harbour in the storm
Just for the broken-hearted
With colours soft and warm

It would welcome many people
Abandoned and abused
A sanctuary, a haven
For egos that are bruised

A healing refuge specially built
For repairing damaged souls
Designed for simple pleasures
Love and acceptance are its goals

We could choose from many activities
Daily massages or daily hugs
Wonderful inner beauty make-overs
All accomplished without drugs

A work-out cabin complete with
Punching bags, games of darts,
Filled with crayons, clay, and paint
For those prone to express the arts

Using reams and reams of paper
In pictures we could say
Secret feelings that we've kept in
Or we could simply choose to play

With all the many toys and games
Enjoyed in childhood days
With supportive friends around us
We would end our abusive ways

But the best service available
Somewhere to verbally let go
A padded soundproof chamber
Let all the anger and rage flow

A very special kind of bank
Deposit guilt and shame
Withdrawing from the ATM
Affirmations instead of blame

And when our stay is over
The price that we would pay
A healthy start, a happy outlook
A stronger US to find our way

Demons of Old

The World of the Past
The World that I feared
The Demons of old
They're no longer here!

Their torment is behind me
I've laid them all to rest
I thought that they knew better
But it's ME that does know best!

They thought they could break me
Oh, how hard they tried.
From fear, pain, and hopelessness
Most every night I cried!

They challenged my defenses
And haunted all my nights
The misery was endless
I grew weary of the fight!

But way deep down inside of me
Was a part they could not shake
And finally, after 50 years,
My true self is awake!

The Demons now are silent
Their power is deceased.
I took command of my own life.
There's only ME to please!

Fixing The Past

When I was just a little girl
The future I could see
I'll make them give me answers
No more secrets will there be

My body will be big and strong
No longer will I fear
The power will be mine someday
My complaints at last they'll hear

But the child in me was unaware
How long it all would take
The journey had its twists and turns
So many bumps, so much heartache

I had failed to make allowance
For the passage of the years
The toll the waiting would exact
As I hid most of my tears

When at last it came to me
I was almost 51
The day all secrets were revealed
I could finally say, "Now, I've won!"

I've found out all you've kept from me
And it's healed most of the pain
You caused by being secretive
My spirit's soaring higher than a plane

But my victory is bittersweet
For the past is done and gone
And now it's best to let it rest
Put it behind me and carry on

The sorrow and the bitterness
In part they still remain
But I'm daily thanking God
At least there's no more pain!

Healing Childhood Trauma

I'm going on a journey
One I started long ago
I've got to make a new life
So my Inner Child can grow

She got stuck in my childhood
Her needs have been denied
Although my body's aged
I'm a little girl inside

What must I do to reach her?
There's so many wounds and fears
I must ask her to reveal
Private thoughts she's held for years

The problem seemed enormous
Just what was I to do?
By chance I found an angel
Who warmly said, "I'll teach you!

You start at the beginning
With patience and with love
With baby steps and day by day
With Spirit's guidance from above"

At first the child was wary
She's learned how not to trust
Because she's hurt for far too long
Allowing her time to heal's a must

The first task that was required
Scared me so bad I wept
She said I had to now reveal
All of the secrets that I'd kept

"You must release those feelings
You've got to have the pain
That's the only way to recover
And be that loving child again!"

My heart and head were pounding
My soul was filled with dread
A warning sounded in my mind
It said, "Tell them and you'll be dead!"

The second task was equally hard
I needed to confront my fears
They had to be at last unearthed
From tombs they'd hidden in for years

At times I had some chest pains
The panic was so immense
I found it hard to concentrate
The depression was so intense

But the hardest task of all
I was so surprised to find
Called for me to cast off my guilt
In order to find peace of mind!

I thought this chore impossible
There were challenges every day
That wounded child in me cried out
"Won't you please show me How to play!"

Relentlessly I reached out to her
Month after month we talked
And when the pressure was too much
We held one another and rocked

The changes, they came slowly
And sometimes I did fall
That's when I became discouraged
"Is there no end to this at all?"

I searched to find some solace
Others' stories touched my heart
Each made new revelations
As old beliefs just fell apart

Finally after five long years
The rewards started to unfold,
A wondrous vision of Spirit,
All of my secrets had been told

I presently have my answers
I've let go of the past
Through rituals of closure
I am healing now at last!

Heart & Soul

When I was just a little girl
I always kept unto myself
But as I grew I became inspired
By the books upon my shelf

Reading other people's stories
Be they real or fictionalized
Studying how they expressed feelings
Was instrumental in opening my eyes

I'd had no words to properly depict
Thoughts and emotions that I hid
Getting lost within the characters
Gave a voice to my inner kid

So now I relate my rendition
Using descriptive poetry and rhyme
The many insights and amazing healing
That I have experienced with time

Being as candid as I can
Talking from my heart and soul
Helping others to find peace and joy
Is now this angel's earthly goal

Her Story

She sits in the shadows
Reading her book
Making notes of feelings
With a far-away look

A song on the radio
Touches her soul
Long-hidden emotions
Give her a new goal

Find new words to express
The inner turmoil
Childhood nightmares repressed
Buried under consecrated soil

Her little girl memories
And tormented heart
Emotional trauma recalled
A mind torn apart

By Dissociative Disorder
A personality split
4 fragmented copies
Puzzle pieces that don't fit

The adult she is now often
Breaks into tears
As words depict old hurts
She relives chronic fears

Determined to tell her story
She's not quite sure how
Is anyone really interested?
Can she help somebody now?

Hours of intense therapy in
The 5 years it took
To integrate the little ones
She could write her own book!

Instead she pours her heart out
Hours at a time
Describing profound images
Making sure the stanzas rhyme

She tells about the loneliness
The suffering, the shame
A battered and bruised self-image
It's all part of the game

That the mind has to play
Just to daily survive
Can you ever understand
The price she paid to stay alive?

"Don't give in to impulses to
Toss it all away
Death's NOT your salvation
You must find another way

Your true path WILL be shown
When you least expect
All questions WILL be answered
You ARE deserving of respect!"

Her whole life she's been bombarded
With this spiritual refrain
Believing that it's Heaven sent
Kept her from going insane

Now exhausted by the effort of
Trying to "get it right"
She gives in to the moment
And retires for the night

Beauty On The Beach

A misty rain tickles my toes
Half a rainbow's in the sky
I giggle and look up as
White, wispy clouds sail on by

The birds are singing gaily
The children are at play
A good song's on the radio
I can sit and relax all day

The buffets are never ending
I've got all that I require
For rest and meditation
Nothing else do I desire

So here on the beach lounge
I spend all of my time
Contemplating peace, and happiness
And putting thoughts to rhyme

I am writing for the lonely
Those filled with tears and pain!
In hopes that I can help them find
Beauty in their life again!

Happiness Is

The feeling is so fleeting
Keeping track's so hard
When trouble overwhelms us
Perhaps we need to make a card

Describing joys and wonders
Those moments too soon forgot
Simple, everyday pleasures
Here's some of the list I got

The soothing sound of music
Fireworks, cuddling with a pet
Traveling to Barbados or Aruba
A colourful, tropical sunset

A cool breeze on a warm day
Or a warm one when it's cool
Rainbows, birds, and butterflies
An in-ground backyard pool

A new book by a favorite author
Powdered sugar on thick French toast
A surprise call from a close friend
Getting support when you need it most

Flowers, solving a hard puzzle
Crystals shining in the sun
Relaxing in a scented bath
When at last the day is done

Party decorations, a recovering pet
Receiving a well-earned compliment
Having something to look forward to
Being given the red-carpet treatment

My personal list's 7 pages long
And it's growing every day
Appreciate all the wondrous little things
Spirit continuously sends your way.

Night Time

There's a mist in the air
Not a breeze to be found
The crickets are chirping
There's no one around

The water's so warm
It's calming me down
And soothing my nerves
So peaceful the sound

The night is so dark
No stars in the sky
Every once in a while
A plane flies on by

I lay by the pool
Just taking it in
The silence and peace
Replacing the din

I'm feeling so light
My soul is at rest
Communing with God is
The time I like best

Tears Of Joy

A wondrous and strange feeling
My body is in shock
A little glimpse of paradise
Secret doors I can now unlock

Yielding to constant enticements
Daring to enjoy life once again
Exquisite dreams of heavenly peace
My heart sings out a new refrain

I wander down the Healing Road
So different from the past
In spite of bumps and potholes
My true soul's free at last

The first few steps are shaky
Awareness happens very slow
Gradually the seeds of happiness
Take root and start to grow

Beginning with a simple smile
That turns into a grin
Taking note of simple pleasures
Quiets the frenzied inner din

Releasing life-long burdens
Allowing my spirit to fly
Surrounded by supportive friends
It's now tears of joy I cry

The Perfect Day

Big, white, fluffy clouds
In a powder-blue sky
Small birds gaily singing
As time flies on by

The sweet smelling flowers
Cool drinks on the beach
Warm breeze all around me
Good book within reach

As nature surrounds me
Without fear and regrets
I'm gratefully happy
My spirit's at rest.

Loving Tributes

Alberta – A Spiritual Journey

Big fluffy white clouds
In a powder blue sky
Acres and acres of farmland
As the miles roll on by

There's a calmness and beauty
That brings peace of mind
A kind of serenity
That's not easy to find

As the bus shifts and sways
I relax in my chair
With a song in my heart
Out the window I stare

The grasslands change to forests
As further south we go
The gently rolling landscape
The hills both high and low

And way off in the distance
They're almost out of sight
The Foothills of the Rockies
With peaks of snowy white

I'm travelling from Edmonton
To Calgary you see
From one soul-mate to another
My Angels both need me.

For Alice

One of my Guardian Angels
Has moved away from me
She's off on an adventure
Her job here done, you see

She's been around for quite a while
Off and on for twenty years
With her loving, caring ways
She calmed most of my fears

I owe her so much gratitude
She taught me how to trust
My feelings and my instincts
And that to reach out is a must

To her, I found, I could reveal
The thoughts I used to hide
And, even more importantly,
She held me while I cried!

She gave me opportunities
To share nurturing and love
As we both sought to understand
His messages sent from above

At times I'd seek her council,
A refuge from the storm
At others, it was she who'd need
An Angel in human form

Now, once again our paths do part
Each goes her separate way
But we know that in the future
They'll cross again some day

Just Like Mom

Childhood fantasies of long ago
A ghostly shadow I long to know
Visions of a phantom in my head
Confronting reality is what I dread

Our journey's end, a pot of gold
Long-kept secrets now can be told
A sister gasps, bids her brother to come
"OH MY GOD! SHE'S JUST LIKE MOM!"

The way she looks, her smiles so great
She's even got most of her traits
But for myself I need to see
Wow! Her picture's just an older ME!

With trembling hearts and souls in shock
Our eyes meet as our hands interlock
In character we are as one
Enjoying collecting and doing crafts for fun

Our little baby souls both still prevail
Our song of suffering a life-time wail
We tell the same jokes, have the same laugh
Being lost to each other tore us both in half

Our likes the same, she dislikes what I do
Music and singing mutual past times too
We wear the same clothes, enjoy the same food
And mimic determination not to intrude

Our will to survive was incredibly strong
50 years apart, convinced in Hell we belong
The curse is lifted, Heaven's come into sight
As adopted child and birth mother at last reunite

M & M

You were the one who gave me life
Though together we could not be
Many times I thought of you
And prayed one day you I'd see

Although I didn't know you well
Whereas we'd only just met
When I found out that you had died
I just broke down and wept

For all the hardships you'd been through
And all things left undone
For the family you left behind
Your daughters and your sons

I pray to God that you've found peace
And for guidance from above
'Cause Mom, when all is said and done
You've always had our love

But now, the truth we each must face
That the special place in our hearts
That we reserved for only you
Hurts like Hell now that we're apart

Mom's Gone!

She was strong and overbearing
And made her opinions known
Her concern for me was genuine
Though perhaps not properly shown

A mother's love is powerful
The bonds that tie are strong
I don't dare try to oppose them
They've ruled for far too long

What will I do without her?
How to live from day to day?
An emptiness engulfs me
Now that she has passed away

We didn't always get along
Some fights went on and on
Oh God! It's so hard to believe
That she is really gone!

So much responsibility
So many decisions now to make
Enormous strength is required
To get me through this heartache

I give thanks for my close friends
On their judgment I rely
Their love and understanding
Comforts me even as I cry

I know that Mom's not really gone
Her spirit surrounds me still
I hear her words, I see her face
I wish there were a pill

To take away the pain I feel
A star to light my way
As I focus on a new routine
With God's help I'll be okay

My Spring

Most people love this time of year
I find it bittersweet
Though it represents life renewed
All I see are the empty seats

A brand new cycle is begun
'Tis the season I was born
But reminders of the ones I've lost
Leads my grieving heart to mourn

As from the winter we recover
With family and friends we celebrate
But the list grows ever shorter
So many "mothers" now are "late!"

The first, my adoptive mother
Her battle with cancer, so long
From one spring to another
Her will to survive was strong

My world revolved around her
She gradually became weak and frail
The emotional horror of her passing
My heart and soul scream out a wail!

The search for her took 50 years
I knew her briefly for only 2
She died Easter Friday morning
Now I've lost my birth mother too!

She was the one I looked like
Possessing my genetic history
It was the healing of our meeting
That led me to create my poetry

And then just two years later
My husband lost his precious mom
The mother-in-law chair's now vacant
So much heartache leaves me numb

On those sunny and warm spring days
That make your spirit take wing
I savor each marvelous moment
And honour their memory, above everything

Pets
and
Nature

Brandy

A tiny white puppy
The size of a mouse
The heart of a lion
The run of the house

Two little black eyes
As cute as can be
His cries won my heart
As he imprinted on me

To him, I was mommy
To me, he was love
A bundle of joy
An angel from above

We had a special bond
That only we could share
A kind of mental telepathy
A silent link, so very rare

Even as the years passed
Though we lived far apart
Our love never faltered
Two souls joined at the heart

I think of him often
And whisper a prayer
"Thank you God for placing
An angel under my care!"

A loving and devoted friend
From 16 to 27
Rewarded for a job complete
He rejoins God in Heaven

Divine Love

They lit up my life
As the stars do the sky
One after another
Till I had to say 'bye.

I'd stare into their eyes
And they into mine
A loving connection
I always did find.

I knew by their actions
That they felt it too
It made me believe that
My dreams could come true.

They did not care about my looks
Not big, nor plain, nor fat.
They gave of their love freely
I was surprised by that.

They lay by me when I was ill
Or when ever I was sad.
And in my lonely, friendless world
They were all the comfort I had.

They were my Spirit Angels
sent down from Heaven above.
I could not have lasted all those years
Without their precious love.

Although they were not human
Those furry friends of mine
They were the answer to my prayers
Proof of His love, divine.

Fallen Friends

As I dwell upon the past
And the special ones I still love
I smile and shed a tear
For they're all angels up above

They came to me in many forms
With a different purpose to fulfill
Each one touched my spirit
Their love fortified my will

I remember every first time
The day each came into my life
The happy and the sad times
How they eased my pain and strife

Some relationships were so short
All too soon they went away
While others lasted many years
I'd always dread that final day

To say "good-bye" is so hard
"Why do we have to be apart?"
Though they're out of sight and touch
They all live within my heart

When sadness overcomes me
I call up a kindred soul
We mourn each other's losses
Telling both our stories is our goal

As time and life go on and on
Again I need someone to hold
In honour of the fallen ones
I welcome a new one into the fold

Over The Rainbow Bridge

It's just outside of Heaven
Where the deceased may choose to wait
For cherished ones left behind
To be joined at a later date

They came into my life
Almost by chance or fate
A haven they could not find
At 5 months old 'twas getting late

Most people want a baby
And they were now half-grown
My daughter and her friend felt
I would give them a good home

I named the white one Armand
Because he liked to bite
His brown brother I named Damien
They were alike as day and night

For Damien he was gentle
And even liked to kiss
But now they're both angels
And their antics I do miss

Perhaps they've linked with other pets
Who've been gone for several years
Believing we will be re-connected
Is enough to bring me to tears

There's quite a list of departed souls
Of many sizes and variety
Hamsters, rabbits and ferrets
7 dogs and a Shetland pony

Treasured moments of life and love shared
Special bonds that will never die
And still the list gets longer
For each new friend tells me why

My Faith and Hope get stronger
With the passing of the years
That so many angels await me
Calms ALL of my darkest fears

My latest is name Sybil
My comfort that she's found
Both Damien and Buzzy
As down the road they all bound

When I make my way to Eden
As lost loved ones and I reunite
We hug and cross the Rainbow Bridge
Forever together, we go into the light

INSPIRATIONAL

and SPIRITUAL

Bless The Angels

How do you bless the Angels?
They gave me back my life.
With patience, with love, with tenderness,
They freed me from my strife!

It was no easy task, mind you.
I fought them all the way.
But when the war was over
We all went out to play!

And now, perhaps, it's my turn
To help someone that way
To help them find the strength they need
To face another day!

To show them they are cared for
It's what we all deserve.
And when you, too, become an angel
Your Higher Spirit you will serve.

God's Embrace

Message of the spirit books
Do just what E.T. did
Open up your heart light
Come out from where you've hid

As I struggle to overcome
A lifetime of hurt and fear
New insights are revealed as
Inner darkness starts to clear

It started as a peaceful dream
That continued when I woke
The answer to my prayers
As with my God I mentally spoke

I feel you in my pounding heart
And it's bursting forth with glee!
I've become so light and peaceful
Since You've lovingly embraced me!

The tears that fell from pain
Now freely flow with joy!
You tell me "**This Is My Love**"
All I can answer is "**Oh! Boy!**"

"**I never gave up Hope**"
Nor I for I had (my daughter)Faythe(Faith)
"**She was my gift to you**"
I know, she's my saving Grace

An angel sent from Heaven!
A sign from up above!
Yes! That's it! Exactly!
A symbol of my Love!

And now it's clear, I'm really blessed
I've found my way back home
And now that You and I are one
Never more shall I roam!

Life's Journey

Communing with Spirit
A dialogue sublime
An answer to my prayers
His message throughout time

"Why did it take so long
For You to come to me?"
"We both were just not ready.
You had to learn! To see!

You had to take life's journey
Far, far away from Me
You wanted to experience
The joy of being FREE!

You had to do this on your own
There was no other way!
But I was there to guide you
When ever you went astray!

'Twas My job to be teacher
'Twas yours to experiment
With the different possibilities
That your mind did invent.

Somewhere along the journey
The roles switch, as you'll see!
You, now, become the teacher
As you tell all to Me!"

The Strength to Endure

Please, let me tell you
About the world that I knew
The hopeless and terrifying
Hell I came through!

The dark, lonely nights
The heartbreaking days
Alone against the world
Have I fallen from grace?

What was my crime?
What did I do?
Am I really so different
From you and you and you?

Although just a child
I had mountains to move
Afraid the accusations
One day I would prove!

Oh! How many times
Can one child's heart break
Before it cries out loud
"No more can I take!"?

The tears that I wept
The pain that I knew
Deep down in my soul
They grew and grew and grew!

Your taunts never ending
Your glances – so cold
"I want it all back,
The childhood you stole!"

Oh! Please make it end
I want a new life
One without terror,
And struggle and strife!

No one did I trust
My thoughts I did hide
Why was there no God
To stand by my side?

Where did my strength come from?
"Am I blessed or am I cursed?"
From whence came the power
To get me through the worst?

Was it Spirit's love I heard?
A pleading voice in my mind
That urged me to endure
"Someday peace you will find!"

Although it took me 50 years
To find my chosen path
I now can say those glorious words
"I am finally free at last!"

I'm finding Spirit's presence
In small and simple ways
And if you ask for guidance
You'll hear Him every day!

ASSORTED

POETRY

A Mother's Love

"Is that what you really think of me?"
Was my daughter's reply.
I can't believe she doesn't know.
Her doubt makes me want to cry.

"I love you more than I can say.
You mean the world to me!
No one has ever touched my soul
The way you have, you see!

Flesh of my flesh, blood of my blood,
You're my own first blood-family.
I look at you and what I behold
Is everything I ever wanted to be!

Do you not know what I think of you?
You always make me feel so proud!
Though this feeling's sometimes hard to express
I would gladly shout it out loud!"

A Special Friend

I met a special friend today
It came out of the blue
I simply walked in through the door
He said, "Hi, my name is Lou!"

I felt I'd known him all my life
Instantly comfortable and at ease
He listened while I told my tale
A good audience, eager to please

Though I'm now more than middle-aged
There's only been a select few
That I could without fear or shame
Completely open myself up to

I'd actually come out to visit
An old friend, my very first
Found a brand new kindred spirit
Quenching a personal life-time thirst

He was as amazed as I was
For a joyful link, brand new
We have a lot in common
We're even the same age too

Over the course of 5 days
And much to our surprise
We're both pupil and teacher
Mutual healing is our prize

This meeting was not happenstance
I believe it spiritually arranged
Though we continue down different paths
Our lives were forever changed

Bullied

A child's psyche is fragile
It changes on a whim
Every time you tease her
When you poke fun at him

All they want is to be friends
An elementary request
Why then are they treated
As if they are but a pest?

Picked on for their differences,
Imperfections, and defects
What cost to their self-esteem
When it's their looks their peers reject?

For something out of their control
Through no fault of their own
They're catalogued and branded
And so the seeds are sown

The consequences can be dire
If this goes on for years
Creating damaged self-images
As the world ignores their tears

The saying goes that words don't hurt
But that is not correct
The wound is to the spirit's core
Almost impossible to detect

But outwardly the signs are there
One only has to care
In silence and in solitude
They hide behind vacant stares

The impact is disastrous
How can they stop the pain?
Should they lash out in rage
Or turn it inward once again?

Facing thoughts of suicide
Needing suffering to depart
Some contemplate a massacre
Revenge for wounds to the heart

Who's responsibility
For dealing with their plight?
Why does no one lend a hand?
I know it can't be right

That parents, teachers, and the school
Ignore what's going on
With no accountability
For cruel deeds that are done

I wish that for one moment
The ones who taunt and jeer
Were transformed into their prey
Hearing what their victims hear

To view first hand the evidence
Of the misery they've induced
Would it possibly change their conduct
If a new perception was produced?

I know this might sound harsh
As for satisfaction we scream
To put them on the receiving end
That's every victim's dream

Feeling Tired

Watching, as the rain pours down
Bouncing, as it hits the ground
Matching the pounding in my head
I really should have stayed in bed!

I'm just so tired that I can't think
Feel as if I need an alcoholic drink
Then maybe I won't feel the pain
As I put myself down, once again

It has that old familiar ring
"Come on! Get going!, and DO SOMETHING!
How can you just sit around all day?
There's work to do! You can't only play!"

Why should I feel guilty and ashamed
Even when the reason can't be named?
When I am feeling so under the weather
Unable to even lift a feather

Why do I feel that I am lazy
If I'm feeling tired and hazy?
Am I not allowed to be sick or ill?
"Who else is going to pay those bills?"

God help me if this feeling lasts
After two days it still hasn't passed
My "inner critic" starts to rant
"Stop saying to me – BUT I CAN'T!"

"Oh! Please! Shut Up! For Heaven's Sake!
I utterly refuse much more to take!
I'm really doing the very best I can
That's all that's expected in God's Daily Plan!

I Am The Wind Beneath Your Wings

Did you ever really know
Who I truly was to be?
The one who gave you strength
From the day you adopted me

I gave direction to your life
Was an answer to your prayers
And made us all a family
Just like your friends had theirs

I felt I was the parent
My job to help you grow
I missed out on my childhood
Though you didn't seem to know

My needs always came second
Your needs always came first
I hid inside your shadow
At times I felt so cursed

I rarely heard a "Thank You"
But I always did my best
To please and make you proud
Never daring to be a pest

Did you know you were my heroes
The ones I looked up to
But you kept all of the praise
And dreams for only you

It took all my power and faith
To get me through the years
As you took all of my love
But refused my fears and tears

Since you both have gone to Heaven
Now that my job is done
I can let my soul take wing
Find my own place in the sun

Kindred

Over and over I imagine
All my dreams are coming true
No longer would I be alone
Never more would I be blue

I cannot find the words I need
For feelings this intense
They overwhelm my spinning mind
Their power's so immense

I've had this hunger all my life
And I don't know what to do
I've even sacrificed my soul
In the hopes that I'd found you

The ones that I belong to,
Other creatures just like me
Who'd welcome me with open arms
Though all my secrets they could see

But still the days and weeks do pass
Nowhere can you be found
I catch a glimpse, I feel you near
My heart, it starts to pound

With you I could be happy
My soul would be at peace
And this mighty, enduring torture
At last would forever cease

At times I grow quite weary
This journey's way too long
My faiths in your existence
Oh God! Could I be wrong?!

I cannot bear to think such things
My heart can't take the pain
The will to live would soon die out
And my mind would go insane!

This fear is overwhelming!
My hope turns to despair!
No longer can I tolerate
My world if you're not there!

I need to believe you're out there
And that some day we will meet!
I need you to embrace me
For my life to be complete!

Making Lists

Take some time to make some lists
They'll help to guide your way
They'll give you hope and comfort
As you struggle through each day

There are many kinds to choose from
Each with a different theme
One thing that I can guarantee
They're more important than they seem

The more that you re-read them
The stronger you will feel
With insights and inspirations
You'll slowly start to heal

So here's the list that I've compiled
I hope that it's a start
But you can choose any ones you want
Ones that speak to your heart;

Affirmations: positive thoughts
Self-Nurturing: self care
Pleasure Activities: fun to do
What Makes Me Happy
Mastery Activities: jobs to do – list them then
simplify the tasks into small steps
Support System: people to call

My Body Is Not Me

When you take a look at me
At my physical frame
What is it you perceive?
I'm much more than a name

Do you find me pretty or handsome?
Do you envy the way I look?
Well, I am here to tell you
The cover does not make the book!

I find that I am burdened
By my bodily imperfections
And others seem to only view
A reason for rejection

They come to the conclusion
Based solely upon their sight
About the kind of person I am
Then conclude that they are right

But I am NOT my body
And my body is NOT Me
My soul is merely housed inside
It's something you can't see

The pretty ones can be dangerous
The ugly can be so kind
There's really not one way to tell
So better keep an open mind

Judge not solely on appearance
But based on words and deeds
Or you may just find you end up
Turning your back on friends you'll need

The Power of Words

Ancient saying goes like this
Words are mightier than the sword
Without them all is silence
Their impact's not to be ignored

With the power to save or kill
To make our feelings known
Written for all to see or
Hidden inside, not to be shown

A frightened and distressed mind
No words to articulate
Daily torment or darkest fears
Alone in a word of self-hate

Her salvation lies in kindness
Words of comfort grant parole
To release the inner turmoil
To nourish her ravenous soul

Their cruel and thoughtless teasing
Reverberating in her head
No hope of being accepted
She nightly wishes she was dead

The constant peer rejection
Wounds the ego and the id
Manifesting as guilt and shame
Cruel curse in the eyes of a kid

How can she possibly express
Scabbed over scars upon her core?
With her throat closed from the pain
Head's thrown back in silent roar

Just when ready to give up
Sweet salvation comes her way
The words she'd only dreamed of
But believed no one would say

"I understand your sorrow
I too have felt that pain
You no longer are alone
And NO, you're NOT insane!"

'Twas their unspoken message
Often repeated in her youth
Angelic memos exorcised
The ghosts to reveal the truth

God whispers encouragement
Teaching us to love His goal
Spiritual tidings cradle
Shattered hearts and injured souls

What Evil Is

I read a book some years ago
The star was quite upset
He believed that he was evil
"Can't go to Heaven!" he did fret

The dictionary stated that
The meaning was quite clear
To harm any human being
That's a fiendish creature to fear

We say some animals are evil
Though on instinct they do act
To be true to one's own nature
Is not truly evil; that's a fact!

I searched my heart and soul to find
A description of my own
The only utterly evil being
Is MAN, as our history has shown!

One day, as if to prove my point
On September 11 or 911
A horrific act!, a demonic deed!
That would dismay most every one!

Some terrorists decided that
Their resentment should be heard
Though many people would agree
That they're actions were quite absurd

They didn't just target government
Their aim was much more diverse
They marked the general public
And forever changed our universe

I thought I knew what EVIL was
Now I'm positive I know
To destroy so many human lives
To a new level it did grow!

My God! Has Satan finally won?
What's the lesson we should learn
As we stare at television sets
Observing buildings crash and burn?

And now the world cries out in pain
With outrage and anger too
We pray for guidance from above
Oh God! Please help to get us through!

As we deal with this disaster
As our tears build up inside
Don't let them start a 3rd. World War!
For there will be no winning side!

Writing Poems

"How do you write the poems?"
They're always asking me
It's kind of hard to answer them
Okay! Well now, let's see!

I write them down in pencil
A little bit at a time
Line by line, verse by verse
I try to make them rhyme

I start out with a topic
Then list what I should say
I think about the order
And then I'm on my way

Some of them are very short
They take less than a day
Some of them are more detailed
For there's a lot to say

Sometimes the words come easily
I hear them loud and clear
At others they refuse to form
Although they seem so near

And when I feel that I am done
I leave it for a while
Then I re-read and make changes
Until I get a smile

Printed in the United States
By Bookmasters